Timber and Prayer
The Indian Pond Poems

Michael S. Weaver

University of Pittsburgh Press
Pittsburgh • London

The publication of this book is supported by grants from the National Endowment for the Arts in Washington, D.C., a Federal agency, and the Pennsylvania Council on the Arts.

Published by the University of Pittsburgh Press, Pittsburgh, Pa. 15260

Copyright © 1995, Michael S. Weaver

All rights reserved
Manufactured in the United States of America
Printed on acid-free paper

Library of Congress Cataloging-in-Publication Data
Weaver, Michael S.
Timber and prayer: the Indian Pond poems / Michael S. Weaver
      p.   cm. —(Pitt Poetry Series)
   ISBN 0-8229-3873-1 (cl.).—ISBN 0-8229-5554-7 (pbk.)
   I. Title.   II. Series.
   PS3573.E1794T56   1995   94-43085
   811'.54—dc20   CIP

A CIP catalogue record for this book is available from the British Library.
Eurospan, London

The author and publisher wish to express their grateful acknowledgment to the following publications in which some of these poems first appeared: *African American Review* ("Providence Journal VII: Ascensions and Disruptions"); Artist and Influence ("Duke Ellington Plays to His Mistress," "Mass Transit," "Willie 'the Lion' Smith"); *Callaloo* ("A Woman from Fredericksburg"); *Calliope* ("Providence Journal VI: Celebrating the Play"); *5 AM* ("Providence Journal I: Piano and Theory," "Providence Journal III: The Celebrity Club"); *Footwork* ("Bootleg Whiskey for Twenty-five Cents," "Jukebox, 1946"); *The Hampden-Sydney Review* ("Sidney Bechet"); *Indiana Review* ("Christmas, 1941"); *Journal of New Jersey Poets* ("The Blue Ford, 1958," "Elsie's Pearl Necklace," "The Lawn," "Otis's Leather Jacket"); *The Kenyon Review* ("Easy Living," "Pearl Bailey," "The Spanish Lesson"); *LIPS* ("Sub Shop Girl"); *The Maryland Pendulum* ("Duke Ellington Remembers Josephine Baker"); *Obsidian II* ("Hamilton Place," "Harlem Society," "Pool Parlor," "Richmond Roller," "Village Quartet"); *Painted Bride Quarterly* ("The Philadelphian"); *Real News* ("Sir"); *River Styx* ("The Big Bopper," "Tuna Fish"); *The Salmon* ("El Duke O"); and *Seattle Review* ("Dancers," "Providence Journal II: French Conversation").

Paperback cover and title page art: Romare Bearden, *Serenade*, 1969. Collection of Madison Art Center, Madison, Wisconsin, Purchase, through National Endowment for the Arts grant with matching funds from Madison Art Center members. Courtesy of Estate of Romare Bearden. Photo by Angela Webster.

Book Design: Frank Lehner

for Donald Faulcon
1945–1990

Trumpet player
philosopher
friend

As black folk
sometimes visited up north
leaving the children
to mind the farm and themselves,
a couple left their place in South Carolina to go to Harlem.
They told their children,
the meanest little sonsabitches for miles around,
to mind the farm and each other.
The urchins started eating the chickens, killing them
by drowning them in a tub.
They called it
"baptizing."
As children do, they got bored with chicken,
fried, baked, and stewed.
They turned around and started eyeing
Henry the Billy Goat.
Henry chewed steady cause he knew
he was in serious trouble.
"Come on Henry, baptizing time,"
sang the little demons.
"Take me to the water," they chimed,
as they dragged Henry to the tub,
his feet leaving a row like a plough digging the earth.
"In the name of the Father,"
they sang as they wrestled with Henry,
but wrestle was all they could do
cause Henry broke free.
They caught him and dragged him back.
Henry knew it was do or die.
He threw the chirren left and right, up and down.
He bucked like a mule and kicked the oldest boy
so hard in the eye he landed up against
a tree, whereupon he cried out
to set Henry free.
"Let the fool go," he shouted.
"He goin to hell
anyway,
no matter what we
do!"

—ANONYMOUS

Contents

Destinations: Saints and Solitude

Harlem Dreams:
The Chosen City, the Chosen People

Points of Departure:
The Lessons of Kinship

I dreamed with my eyes gazing blankly upon the landscape until I looked up to see a Red Cap frowning down. "Buddy, are you getting off here?" he said. "If so, you better get started."

"Oh, sure," I said, beginning to move. "Sure, but how do you get to Harlem?"

"That's easy," he said. "You just keep heading north."

. . . .

"What I want to know is," he said, "Is you got the dog?"

"Dog? What dog?"

—RALPH ELLISON
Invisible Man

Donald,

I know now that black folk in some parts of the South call the act of prayer "putting up timber." As poetry is prayer, this timber is for you and me, as we know which way is up.

We are, as ever, in the need of prayer.

Christmas, 1941

for Mark Joseph Weaver

My father and his mother
came north on a train
powered by black smoke
billowing back from
an old, huffing engine
that drove its wheels
with relentless metal arms.
He was nineteen,
a big, strapping boy
sprouted from the ways
of a small farm,
raised in the wooden house
that stood twenty-seven years
after this trip to Baltimore,
the wooden house that was
a large box of planks
sitting up on columns
of stones piled and held together
with mortar, the wooden house
that heard the hoorays
when he was born.

His mother's guard and charge,
he sat entranced at the window,
wondering what the city was like,
what groaning blues it kept
in its cheeks like snuff,
what shifting love it held
where people were as thick
as wasps pouring from a nest.

At home the city
was Lawrenceville, a hamlet
he could stand on the edge of
and holler and be heard
on the other side of town,
a sleepy face of a place
with a five-and-dime
and old men in overalls
who blurred the distinction
between country and city,
between unbound and bound.

He reached into the paper box
for another piece of chicken
and met his mother's glance,
taunting and half-stern,
reminding him they had a ways to go
and he looked around to study
the other passengers who
looked back half-friendly
with eyes that sang out,
Go on way from here boy,
Ain't nobody studyin bout you,
or they sang out lovingly
like new grandparents with eyes
that promised to dream along
with him until they were north,
north of the guiding grimace
of Richmond, north of the capital of the North,
Washington, which surprised him
when the train rumbled through it.

In Baltimore his mother eyed him
like a nurse with a blind man,

as the buildings and the traffic
struck him dumb and dazzled,
and his mouth fell open
to suck in the city's liquid magic
that boiled on the notes
of a music of heart upon heart,
conscience upon conscience,
trudging soul upon trudging soul
where people amass to live
and to die together. He forgot
the night bird's song,
the whippoorwill's aria,
and the ripping cut of hot fields
as he walked in a new Jerusalem.

The Blue Ford, 1958

In middle age, a son finds
himself in his father's memories
and hears his father's voice as
his own.

I thought of the miracle
of the V-8 engine when
I remembered the old Ford
the white neighbors had
down home. It was so light
the large wife of this quiet man
had to sit on the opposite end
so it wouldn't turn over
like a bug that awkwardly
gives up its ghost and legs,
or like the vision of travel that
makes you curse and fret.
We eased out of the maze
of Washington, followed
Route 1, the old highway.
The children gazed
at the palaces of white power.

She ran smooth and sure.
She responded to the request
for more torque to be turned
down into the gears to become
the forward surge and glide,
the rush of air against our faces,
the laughter in the children.
Bessie said something
about air conditioning and Cadillacs.

I said it must be foolish
to spend God's summer
in a rolling icebox. It mocks
the Lord, sets in arthritis.
The road began its long dips
up and down hills so steep
the trucks sped like
logs of steel that menaced us.
I glanced at my family, thought of
the death that hungers for travelers.

This was the old day
of the large billboard
and the highway that was a park
that was something to see.
People often wrote home,
Child, that was something to see.
We stopped at an eatery
just on the other side
of Fredericksburg, and
one of the children mentioned Lee.
Another mentioned Lincoln and asked,
"Daddy, would Eisenhower
have freed the slaves?"
I said honestly that it all
has to do with golf,
with scores and the amount of ease
with which the rich and powerful
can promenade through lush fields.
The rich conquer the poor.

The blue Ford beckoned,
and we piled back into it,

sucked on the last ice cream.
The light faded, evening rose.
In the picture of the clouds
I saw the heads of people
move about slowly, position
themselves above and around one another.
Some looked like kin.
Some looked like kind strangers.
The sun fell backwards,
threw up its legs as it went.
It sent yellow shafts in a fan,
like a gifted humpty-dumpty.
I drove carefully into
history's hand, the hand
that dares not to forgive.

Otis's Leather Jacket

for Otis R. Weaver

The brown leather jacket
that stood on the porch,
counted the men who rode
to the steel mills;
that hit the air that
bristled as we drove to funerals
in Virginia and Carolina,
and dared back nostalgia;
that could get tough
with Jersey Joe Walcott
the older Joe Louis,
or Rocky Marciano;
that took me down and away
to the white university
and left me in strangers' gasps,
and hoped for a professional
son to emerge from the bone
glasses and the peanut head;
that came home and ached for Bessie
after she had a full day
with daughters and sons,
with forgive, forget, remember,
with the body's song, its wish
for hot and brief union;
the jacket that came to call itself
time or birth or death,
that hangs in closets now
in a hundred affected lives,
as bones crack and dreams preach.

Elsie's Pearl Necklace

for Elsie "Bessie" Weaver

The fake pearl necklace
that peeped at lovemaking
from its perch on the vanity
of blonde wood bought
from a rich furniture store
in the segregated years;
that went up to school
when they called and said
I was too smart for most things,
not smart enough for the rest,
the important things;
that stopped going to church
when the orders for sainthood
were given out and she was bound
to serve her mother
and guarantee her own shortened years
to tumble down the trail to sleep;
that sang in the mornings
in the house emptied of children,
sang off-key and proudly,
in an enriched cacophony;
that marched up to Dr. Adams
and demanded I be given
a raise to five dollars a week
from two dollars fifty cents,
that confronted the bourgeoisie;
that held my head
when everything crumbled,
and I thought life a cruel trick
designed to enfeeble us all,

until we beg for an ending;
that settled the arrangement
of hate that disguised itself
in blossoms and all is well;
that took love from its dangerous
perch where it could not fly
and set it on the earth;
that gave me cod liver oil
and Milk of Magnesia firmly;
the fake pearl necklace
that secured my emerging faith
and anointed my life.

The Philadelphian

for Sallye Warr

You differ with the wise,
sweeping the crest of light snow
from your face and the front steps.
You cast a lightning eye
to the sky, remember the silhouette
of clouds in North Carolina,
remember the southern song
of your father carrying you aloft,
after hunting for possum and deer.
In nightmares you abandoned southern speech,
like fear's weak eyes trying a melody
away from this southern song, but it lives
inside your very center where you
walk past your mother's elocution,
pretending to be gaunt, grim—proper.

I'm a mean, tall gal from Carolina.

On the way to the el, you count
the many intonations of words you savor
as much as ice cream or pound cake,
for the way they march off your tongue
like dynamos in Saks Fifth Avenue suits,
the appropriate appearance,
the apportioned approval.
You trade again for *agane.*
You trade rather for *rahther.*
You have a peculiar preciosity for
the lexicon's omissions, for verbal sloth.
You hold your head erect, recreate

English in your image, your sound.
On the subway you shudder and wince
at the obscenities children assume
are the natural course of language,
language which is so much our birth
and our death. You command
one of them to mind his mouth,
as you tighten your fingers on a bag
that is your carryall, straighten
the sneakers that take you through.

Manners, manners, manners! Hey, selah!

Never mind the weight of regret,
the weight of what could have been.
In the dark evening, the accounting,
the measure of your daylong acculturation,
you measure your refinement in
the darkening of spiced tea hot enough
to scald the initiates entering the rigor
of settling up North as the venerated heads
discussed when you were knee-high to hope—
little Sallye in the cathedral of pine trees,
little Sallye rising from the sour hate,
little Sallye mending the ain'ts and yes ma'ams
that embolden Dixie like spires of lily leaves.
You fall into a Philadelphia sleep,
on the sofa, in your favorite spot,
your head nodding in the city's vast webs,
recalling a cricket's alto in High Point,
as you spin in a homemade dress.

I'm a mean, tall gal from Carolina.
I'm the fortunemaker in my dreams.

The Lawn

for Sean Ruffin McNeill

Saturdays we took out the push mower,
my father in short sleeves with a handkerchief
tied around his neck to catch the sweat.
He came out after he drank coffee in
a kitchen so warm the glossy plaster walls
turned slippery. The smell of sausages
slithered past our noses in waves.

I took his orders. I went for the file
to sharpen the turnstile of blades
that whistled when I gave the mower
a push hard enough to spin the cutters.
They were like a silver cone spinning.
They sometimes caught a bee harvesting
and cut his woolly belly. Full registers
of bee grief went out through the weeds.
A tiny death seized its unconscious prey.

My father took the file and eyed it.
He played the craftsman, sat on our chair
my aunt broke with her quarter ton of love.
He sat there half out of it, leaned over
to see how best to reach the blade that was dull,
the traitor that sat behind the metal bar
and only half pretended to cut the grass.
The grass was both victim and benefactor
of the reaping, of the turning down.

The slow screech and scrape of metal on metal
hassled the nerves of sparrows on the pole

where the clothesline hung from the house
to the edge of the alley. There my mother hung
the bright whites and frail frill of flowers
to dry while she talked to Mrs. Parker or
to Miss Gladys when Mrs. Parker died.
The dreaded drone of the metal sound of death
hit and left that house to strangers.

When it was done, when the filing of blades
left the grim decision to shine so sharp
it drew blood, I pushed the mower out.
I went onto the lawn and it began to sing.
Up and down it sang as it sliced the topmost
portion of the grass. It cut the green down
so that it seemed every single leaf
was the same height, that they could all
begin again somehow. My father lit
his Winston, plucked his ashes on petunias.
My hands toughened on the handle of his mower
that sang out endings and beginnings.

Tuna Fish

for Lucille Clifton

Every day tuna fish,
in every conceivable manner.
With tomatoes that leaked
and made the bread soggy,
with lettuce my mother tore
in odd shapes that hung
like ornaments from my mouth
in the cafeteria, the high court.
I had tuna on toast toasted lightly
that was death-cold at noon,
on toast toasted darkly
that crumbled like old ruins
just when I was in front
of LaRue Ashe. She always
wanted to kiss me long
before I knew why she
was so proud of the French
in her name.

Tuna in waxed paper
that tore and fell on the floor,
tuna in aluminum foil
shaped like flying saucers
that we threw at each other
in assassination attempts.
Tuna from brand names,
Star-Kist that always rejected
hip Charlie in the sunglasses,
Bumble-Bee with its
oxymoron soul of insects and fish.

Tuna made the day before,
which seemed to smell
truly like dead fish, the dead fish
killed by pollution and washed up
like rejected never-to-be's,
the dead fish of hot sun.
And nothing was so obviously poor
as eating this when other kids
had hot spaghetti from the kitchen
where women like my mother
labored over shiny pots and steam.

Nothing was so distinctly humble
as munching tuna and mayo
when LaRue Ashe mounted
the bench of the table
like the acrobat she was
and asked aggressively for a kiss.
I sat as stupid
as a confused cat, blinked,
masticated the sea's journeyman,
bemoaned my banal lunch,
but dreaded the deeper pit
of despair, tuna's alter ego,
bologna. I knew full well
and grievously that LaRue
could never come to view
bologna as romantic. I knew
perhaps unconsciously that few
meats are as seductive as fish.

Science

One day you'll be a credit to your race.
—Mrs. Moody

From behind your tableau,
bunsen burners, beakers, test tubes,
with the periodic table for
mise-en-scène, you measured
my light's luminescence and clarity.
You missed the obvious truth.
I meditated with reverent eyes
on a man descending with open arms
and flowing hair and robe from
the boisterous beginnings of words.

You commanded me to hold a snake.
It was a black snake that wiggled
like rubber. I prayed for God's voice
to announce an intervention.
I thought it would be a still voice
like the one to Elijah and Samuel,
or like the soothing annunciation.
El Shaddai, God of my fathers,
Eli, Eli, Lord of junior high school,
rescue me from this snake
that slinks and slithers, rescue me
from Mrs. Moody's science class.

I prayed before and after every class,
to take away this snake that I feared.
Eyes sometimes closed, sometimes open,
my lips pursued the English of King James.
I didn't understand the sex of it all.

Sub Shop Girl

for James "Eddie" Mann

She is lovely. Her eyes are big almonds
floating over the electronic cash register.
She puts magic dust in my mayonnaise,
hoochie-koochie notes in my fries.
There is no other reason to order
tomatoes, lettuce, hot peppers, onions,
and french fries in a suit and tie.
I come nearer the shop tiptoeing in Florsheims.
With a quarter I set the mood on the jukebox.
"What do you want today?" she asks, "What is it, Baby?"
I am probably the only man who puts strategy
in a Saturday night foray to the sub shop.
I line my cologne up carefully on the dresser,
the Parisian designer bottle for cheese steak,
for pizza the cheaper, less subtle aromas,
laying my clothes out to match each meal.
She puts the change in my palm a coin at a time,
measuring the contours of the lines in my hands.
I think I lost my sanity a long time ago
on the way to buy a foot-long and fries.
The essence of Shango fires my red urge
longing to meld with the small greasy apron
that throws frozen steak portions with expertise.
How could the heavens have wasted such youth
on me and this corner sub shop and vagrants
and the empty neon in after-hours streets,
and the music from old Smokey Robinson 45's
I play on my boom box the nights I want to serenade?
Have you ever listed the extras on a cold cut with
"Tracks of My Tears" or "Second That Emotion"?

When the shop is closed some Sundays I melt
in the afternoon apparitions in the empty windows,
the deserted counters, the cold ovens, the silence.
There are blessings for noble spirits confined
to ordinary lives, the dribble of an oba like me
and a great spirit like my sub shop Oshun slicing pickles.
There are blessings as we dazzle the ordinary universe,
pervert the threadbare perceptions of doldrums
with our elegant affair at night, our perfect love,
me in an all-leather racing jacket and Gucci loafers.

One night after work I'll coax her and we'll pretend
to be Marvin Gaye and Tammi Terrell on the parking lot.
I'll caress her around the waist and spin her softly.
A dark night sky laden with stars will crack,
the moon will pour love's essence on the earth,
truth will overcome us on the voices of the orishas—
"Ain't Nothin Like the Real Thing Baby," or maybe
"You're All I Need to Get By," but most of all the song
the world needs to hear—"You Ain't Livin Till You're Lovin."
I am probably the only man who sees the answer
in a cheese-steak hoagie with all the fixins and fries,
music from my boom box or the jukebox nearby,
two almond eyes as deep as canyons over the counter,
and my Gucci and Florsheim shoes doing a soft tap,
the mania and danger of an insecure world hanging out
like a florid design in the curtain of the night.

A Woman from Fredericksburg

for Lenora R. Davis

The blade of the mower sliced your toe
on a day otherwise unremarkable,
sliced your big toe and sent it bouncing
like Marie Antoinette's head from
the heavy, sliding guillotine,
painfully like your first daughter
who came bright, high, and even.
You took your toe with you
to the hospital before microsurgery
could amend your abrupt amputation,
despite your knowledge of medicine
you dispensed on Saturday afternoons.
You leaned back against the sink's counter,
smiled so that your mole beneath
your eye stood in bold relief, smiled
to explain some principle of biochemistry.
Impromptu lecturer, you made
your mark when you escorted a nephew
of your soon-to-be husband to
Walter's Art Gallery in downtown Baltimore,
where the wealthy come for lunch,
in the midst of the city's old-world flavor.

You took him round and around,
waited for his world to open up
and admit the light to guide his light,
which you suspected burned difficultly
inside him. You watched and talked,
explained Leonardo da Vinci's genius,
because you knew how much this boy
loved machines but also that he had
an artist's sense of the delicate, the frail.

Always the talker, always the savant,
your voice sang through the garden
at cultivation time under the heat.
Hoes moved up and down beside you.
The horses stood bemused in the shade.
You chattered on about classical education,
about the strength of black colleges
in the South that trained legions
of doctors, lawyers, teachers, ministers,
and consummate intellectuals like you.

That one stout and frail nephew
worked beside you in near silence,
stopped to punctuate your speeches
with his insight won from his own books,
his own private hours of study and reflection,
not unlike your beginning. You wore on
until it was too hot to work, when the grass
let out its shrill mourning in stillness.
You trudged up the hill past
the old garage which was torn down,
on the hilltop where the house stood
as sentinel over your Arabian horse farm,
and where, years later, the mower
took your toe while you were not looking.
You thought instead, for one fearful minute,
of something else, some other thought
that connected to the progression
issued from the source of your mind,
that invisible point you sought to affect
in the young, the faintly promising.
You empowered them as makers and healers.

The Big Bopper

Ernie always came back with pictures,
after a weekend with the women
at a cabaret or in a club.
In his snapshots he stood in the middle,
sported a new outfit. His smile
shot out from his false teeth
in a bright flash. We could not see
the awkward pain of the skin lesions
on his face. The scars made people wince
and wonder what sustained his ebullience.

Once he fell from his tractor.
He landed near a pole by the machine
that counted the boxes and packed them
like an obedient slave without hope.
We rushed over to him
as he sat there and held his stomach.
The manager told Stu to take his place.
Clown that he was, Stu sat
at the pole next to Ernie and held
his own stomach, imitating loudly
the sound of pain and humiliation.

Before he went for his operation,
he told me he was afraid
of the cut from sternum to groin,
of hands sliding behind his heart
to repair his esophagus. I told him
it was nothing, that he would come back
on a Monday as usual, to the clock,
to the sameness of our routine.
Soon he would be able again to pull out
some credit cards for one of his women
and buy her a dress to take a picture.

The operation over, he and I spent time
on a veranda in Johns Hopkins Hospital.
We watched women so far away we could not
see their smiles or the fit of their skirts,
only filmy figures that floated away from us.
Everything grew dimmer in the sky.
I came back to tell how he passed.
I knew all Ernie ever wanted was the glamour
and the conviviality of the moment,
even as he glided on the dance floor,
nimbly out of sight.

Salvation

for Donald Faulcon at Lake Montebello

In symbol,
I blow your ashes
over the lake's ripples
that roll in under
the western end
of the world.
Your high tenor,
the sound of wood
that is cut to burn,
crackles. Your ashes
draw a body that
dissipates, lives
only for an instant.
The ashes spread
from tip to tip.
You claim
an eternal deed
on the place we believed
we would always
return to, until
the last second.
I pray that
you can hear
my wish where
you have command
of the light
that illumines my grief.
I pray that you can
see me where
all human futility

is spun like funny silk
on a wisdom's loom.
I pray that you can
laugh and mimic my laugh
in a private corner
like the space where
our lives intersected.
I am now alone
in the mind's
recounting of itself.
Life flips backward.
From the ashes,
a chip of bone
remains, rattles
in the urn. It is
the valley's single
icon of rebirth.
I take the bone
in my hand
to feel the definite,
to feel the imprecise.
I remember this is a day
like any other day
when we understood
a philosophy or a creed,
and the lake drank
our laughter as comic
or as congenial and wise
as where we begin
or where we end
this collecting
we call a life.

El Duke O

for David Johns

His hands ache in white gloves
on twin silver canes that wobble.
His eyes pull over the wall of sadness,
peep to recognize hope's allies,
and the voice, the rickety voice—
Flip, flop, and fly.
    I don't care if I die.

In the busy audience,
a woman in a black turban,
a smile like New Orleans,
love like Rocky Mountain,
eyes that remember old lives,
lives now gone from applause's chatter,
from the holler, from the shout—
Kiss me and hold it
    until it's sweet as wine.

He careens on the end of life,
his face captured in a photograph
that sits on the piano, his publicity.
He announces to the novice,
those that don't know the body's treason,
the encyclopedia of pain that opens
to souls that never dreamed of ache—
You look like a Mississippi bullfrog
    sitting on a hollow log.

Moving away from his piano with its keys,
he glances at the woman in a black turban.
He shuffles through memory's membranes,

forgets the act of forgetting,
remembers his hopes for fame.
He eases to the door in an old cashmere,
the angel of love in whiskers.
He shuffles out into a Saturday night—
Don't ever leave me.
   Don't ever say bye bye.

High Sierra

I take my Schwinn High Sierra bicycle
down the gravel road through the woods.
I am afraid of the physics of speed and hills,
afraid that the whir might become a hush
where the trees, brush, and flowers whisper
a song that wishes away virtual harm.
You warned me of this danger when I abandoned
you in the steel skeleton of the warehouse.
i left my home and my wife, emblems of failure.

The brakes squeak on the steel rims.
They sound like a bird with a broken wing
caught out in the thick undergrowth.
It hopes that no predator, cat or fox,
will find it and rip its weaknesses,
cut it to the bone and beyond to where nothing
is left. What will verify the imperfect memories
that we hope will resurrect the dreams
that took body and then disappeared?
Do all the moments of a life fade
into the scattered conversations of the old?

At the blessed bottom of the hill,
I look back up at the top, where I began.
It eludes me, shifts with shadow,
moves along in alliance with the sun.
I cannot see the sun, its heavy fire.
I circle in the sand on the bottom,
wonder if I have succeeded or failed.
I am not sure if I can pedal uphill,

even with the lowest of my fifteen gears.
They are so low that I am not exercised.

In a northern light away from my southern birth,
I ask you, *my friend the trumpet player,*
may I pretend? *Why do land and love bind?*

A Maxim

I was once accused
of being a perfectionist.
In fact, she said
I tried to be
too perfect, as
just perfect was
not bad enough.
I was secretly proud
of the perfection
of someone who is
too perfect.
The greater secret
was I often felt
that I was unfinished,
just short of the mark.
The mark was always
moved by some manipulator.
After all, this sacred self,
the Hindu brilliant jewel,
is just subjective.
This person who
hung my guilt for
all the world to see
probably just saw in me
something she wanted.
For us perfect folk,
all life coheres.
We are secret egotists.
We worship curves,
the round parts
that make life
more interesting.

The curves are where
mistakes are taken
lightly, taken out
of guilt's crucible.
In perfection,
the perfect wash
themselves in shame,
as my brilliant jewel
catches me smiling
in its perfect mirrors.

Way Stations:
The Changing Habits of Change

Upon their Emergence to this new Fourth World, the people were told that they could not simply wander over it until they found a good place to settle down. Másaw, its guardian spirit, outlined the manner in which they were to make their migrations, how they were to recognize the place they were to settle permanently, and the way they were to live when they got there. All this was symbolically written on the four sacred tablets given them.

—FRANK WATERS
Book of the Hopi

*Met myself on a lonely road,
         found in my eyes a heavy load.*

—ANONYMOUS

Mass Transit

for Sonia Sanchez

She sat at the front
near the driver, watched
as new riders dropped
their change and flashed passes.
She sat stoical and grim
in a dress blue like the passive
colors for a baby boy,
or the blue of peace.
Everyone jostled along
with the creak and moan
of the bus that strained
to fit the contours of earth
like a worm in a straitjacket.

I peeked over the shoulder
of the woman in front of me
to read her Haitian newspaper.
I caught the bold print
in an ad for a get-rich scheme—
Devenez riche maintenant!
She read slowly and intently,
while the rest of us ached
silently for a quiet ride home.
In all this intimacy, we were
thrown together with strangers:
grandmothers who returned
from shopping where merchants
devour the poor,
young women who carried books
home from college,

the community college
where they battled like Marines
for their hope, and me
with my briefcase and poetry,
as I rode back from the law school.
All of us ached
for a quiet ride home.

The woman in blue erupted
but did not change her face.
With the same smile
almost a grimace she said,
"Better get ready for the judgment,
my Lord is coming down."
The bus rattled
over a large pothole as
we all shot up stiffly for a second
and realized she was preaching.
"All this crack and stuff.
Lord don't like it! You all guilty!"
Suddenly she became
what I suspect she wanted to be,
the angel sent in the last hour
before the others come
with their wrecking crew
of pestilence, famine, and war.
They turn a perfect summer day
like this to burning blood
and raise the lake of fire
so that everyone can see
the serpent beat the surface
with his infinite tail.
Her blue became the blue

of some fires that look cool
from a distance, belie
their ability to make the skin
crackle and curl to ash.

The driver picked up speed,
hoped that each stop
would be hers and her sermon
would stop its march up and down
like a rider who intimidates
on the late-night buses,
when the angry old men ride.
But she sat as if riveted
to her seat. Slowly,
the passengers began to thank her
as they got off, those riders
who knew the hour of our condition.
They touched her softly on the knee
and whispered kindly to her,
"God bless you sister."
She smiled and adjusted
her grip on her Bible.

We began to forget
about her and Judgment Day.
We bounced along, braced ourselves
for the awkward crawl
around the corners as we passed
the deserted lots of Newark
and headed into East Orange.
There men in disheveled clothes
gathered near abandoned buildings.
It seemed that doom
had already come with its heralds

and gone. Through it all
I thought of a friend's dispensation
for those traveling the Apocalypse—
"Only the poor ride the bus."

Richmond Roller

for Harry M. Williams

You hid your southern laughter
to roll out the New England phrases
on a tongue used to summer,
used to greens, used to iced tea.
You hid the shamefulness of a drawl
that was only shameful because
here in New England folk think
the vowel "a" is really "ah,"
that it should vibrate the throat
in words like *can* and *band*.
You hid your country savoir faire.

You wrote your dissertation
on George Schuyler, the man
who was no nonsense and no sense,
who believed black people are
just white people in black accoutrements,
a kind of drag costume.
You believed George was human
after all, that he deserved all
of six hundred pages and the five years
you beat around in libraries,
interviewed relevant people,
pasted the particulars of his life
all over your apartment where
you kept your southern soul
in thousands of testimonies.

That day in the library when
you talked to the telephone itself,

not the person you tried to call,
I took you for a walk. I was concerned
that Schuyler had his revenge
on a Virginia homeboy so rich with style
that it made me smile to see you walk,
catch whispers of home when you broke
into that rich vernacular,
as you pushed open the door to the doctorate,
cheered on by fans who loved
your southern sense and taste.

Reunions

for Aissatou Mijiza

The pigeons were mock travelers.
They popped their staccato heads
across the wooden station floor,
as the Amtrak workers studied donuts
and cooling cups of coffee with cream.
I took the lower level walkway to where
the train from New York stops, across
the creaking, old planks of the floor
that is now the basement of a condominium
for Bostonians who can't afford Boston.
The train slid in on its slow electric,
and you stepped down, smiling, inviting
me to the meticulous pluck of the soul
against its own bone, the confessions
of how much we missed each other and why
we even allowed this distance and this travel.
Why did we come to this? Why did we wait
for reunions in the company of strangers?
Why did we travel on trains into
the horizon's gift to coveting, to sadness?

You always packed your entire life
when you went away for a weekend, and
I struggled with your bags to the car.
I pointed out the downtown of Providence.
It is a short scat in a love song
that old men from Portugal croon,
that old women from Cape Verde whisper,
that children from Puerto Rico sing in games.

You ignored it all and asked me to kiss you
out where no one sees or cares except
the awkward sense of history, of slaves
old man Brown bought and sold as fortune
and left in the form of some legal deed
to a parcel of earth. Human life
is nothing if it can't be translated into
legal concepts with a map inscribed
with borders taken from your dreams.
So say the powerful, I explained.
You pulled a gift from your bag, a teddy bear.
I was instantly figured over with lines,
like Gulliver in Lilliput, your love
having converted itself to a million pygmies.

For two days we went on this way.
I entertained the thought of freedom,
and you held me, secure in your power,
satisfied to allow me the mobility
of being led around like the giant
on the cart. You watched the loose eyes
of women young enough to be my daughters
but old enough to promise to restore
my slowly vanishing youth. Innocent,
I seemed to enrage you. Guilty, I seemed
to be as women think men should be,
lusty enough to leave, but content
enough with their beauty to succumb.
The problem with Providence for us
was that there was too much beauty,
and too much of it in love with tragedy.
A man like me could escape there

from the truth of himself he has won
from a lifetime of handling the hosts
behind the eye, behind the thought, where he is
embattled by ideas of life's limits.

When it was time to undo ourselves
from each other, we half apologized
for screaming at each other in the shower.
We agreed it was great to be able to touch
once again. Together we thought wordless
thoughts of how separation can stifle
a thing like we had or we have become.

The Albany Hotel

for Aissatou Mijiza

At Boston I took the train to Chicago,
one full of people looking forward
to sleeping from the Adirondacks to the city
of Wright's and Sullivan's new architecture.
They wanted to awake freshened and alert
where the Mississippi brought the blues to rest.
I tried to imagine Albany when I met a woman
from Bigger Thomas town who sat and read
along with me. She began to share her life,
her troubles, her name, Sally, a rush of strength,
as all the Sallys I have known have shown
themselves to be. We sat together and drank
beer from the café car before she took a seat
to herself so she, too, could sleep into Chicago.
She cautioned me not to study too hard,
invoking the myth of old folks in the South
who believe books can steal your very mind,
and leave you to babble in public places
like Nietzsche or beggars in Manhattan
who startle commuters with eloquent nonsense.
The train pulled into Albany's five-and-dime station,
and Sally gave me her address as I disembarked.

In Albany there is a building that
Rockefeller built for the state's affairs.
If you stand in its often empty plaza,
you can look out to the horizon's expanse,
and you might expect to be aboard a space ship
cruising one of the eighty-eight configurations
of stars, perhaps Orion. For a moment,

you can gaze at these razor-edge buildings
and think we are more advanced than we are,
that our learning has given us this lip to
the galaxy's edge. Then you go down the street
to the humble row houses near the barbershop,
and it all comes back frightfully, like an onslaught
of information you call up when you study.
I checked into the humble and clean hotel,
and I put Sally's address away for later.
I had given her my ear and wanted to keep open
the line to her and to new cities.

I spread the books around on the vacant bed,
and I smiled to think what a lover I had there.
Her voluptuousness lay in the curves
of revelations she walked me to the edge of with
arms that coaxed me into a soft erudition.
I began to anticipate the end of this examination
and the ride back to Boston, with my head
rolling with the train's shifting loll. I heard
some people in another room making love.
I clutched a book and some articles and read on
about what life is or can be. On the phone,
I argued with you so loudly that all the words
around me exploded from the page, from my mind,
from the air of the dead's encapsulations,
and they burst into a canopy of ordered stars.
I realized I had left the sense of a life
and gone over into the abyss where mountains smile
resolutely, and the wind laughs and sings.

Weeks later, back home in Providence,
I received a letter from Sally. She wanted

to hold on as well. She had hopes for me,
and there were words of her life's distress.
She made me think we move on like feet
on Jacob's ladder or smiles at helms of star ships
coursing through the spaces between worlds.

My Son Flies to Visit Me in Providence

for Kala Oboi

You shot past the flight attendant
trying to look worldly, but for all
your sangfroid, you were quite askew.
Twelve and traveling alone,
your shirttail flapping out, collar
hanging over your jacket, buttons
misaligned, shoelaces flailing about.
You were quite terrified
of having flown this far with strangers.
We walked along slowly
through the airport as small
as a K-Mart where passengers
dressed in jeans with cheap bags
waited for flights to the outer world.
They were refugees from the rustication
of Rhode Island with the Mafia,
and the international village of Providence.

I pointed out to you the hill
where the colonials fought back
the British, a hill owned by a slaver.
You were not impressed
by subtleties of lives lived and gone,
and wanted only to know why
at this juncture in your grand design
I had chosen to come here away
from everything we both knew.
I took away the tidy row house near the lake,
afternoons in your room with videos,
Sunday roar of fans from the stadium

where the Orioles lost game after game,
and the hikes through the park.

I remembered regretfully
that you left first, you smashed
the photograph of us standing together
and called your mother, and left.
What are children if they are not
conscious of what they do, even if
they cannot fully see the outcome?
Neither can we with our wealth
of mistakes. So in the vacuum
I left too, left everyone.
I left to recover something lost
long ago when I had more chances.
You wanted to know why
there was such pleasure for me
in a brick room full of books,
as you threw tantrums and begged
the impossible, to be readmitted
into my small space, to be relieved,
but on the last day I sent you back,
agreeing with you mother's wishes.
Sadly, I signed you over to the plane and
to the good graces of Eleanora, my first wife,
who waited, smiling, in our youth.

Providence Journal I:
Piano and Theory

Like a spider in her web,
Our piano teacher sat in the corner
of the final examination room.
Behind a Baldwin baby grand, she sat
with her notebook and her humor
so unpredictable that it poked us
like the hairy legs of a tarantula.
She made our teeth clatter and clink.
She secured the fate of failures
like the awful arachnid that counts limbs
caught in her silk spun and cast
to hold those not sensible enough
to traverse life's gauntlets.
When I came to the last measures,
my faith sank to where it lay flat.
My vision grew blurred and indistinct.
I crawled through a phrase
that took the fingers over themselves.
I passed the final bar, passed the exam,
passed the teacher as she nodded to me
from her chair with fingers as adroit
as the four pairs of legs of Araneida.
She smiled with teeth like crossed spinnerets
that hang lightly between congratulation
and silent murder in the silk.

Providence Journal II:
French Conversation

We never said anything definite,
except to argue over the blues
in the weak French of French class.
We sat in our conversation group
in a café filled with pretenders.
We knew very little for sure except
that you were white and I was black,
that you were thirteen years younger,
that you were used to privilege and fame.
I know now I will not forget your name,
Danielle, where the *l*'s vibrate
like venetian blinds in a soft breeze.
I mentioned B. B. King as a bluesman,
and you said you grew up with the blues.
Your father knew them and played them.
The real blues are bawdy,
bawdy enough to curl the censor's pen.
B. B. King does not hit the core
of the essence of songs about sex and hurt.
We argued in our weak, scholastic French,
not the real French of Paris or even
of the slow farmers in the countryside
who look out over France's low hills,
drink their red wine in the long evenings.

Later we met beside the dormitory.
You introduced me to your father
with a long vita to impress him.
The terror in his eyes curled like whips.
I lost something in your wincing lips,
turned to wonder my way up the street.
I remembered how we wanted something to
go solid and knock deep in our souls.
I thought of the profane avenue to love.

Providence Journal III:
The Celebrity Club

At the balcony we leaned over
to watch the ball in full eruption.
The emcee was in his reserve and white suit.
He came to the microphone in perfect voice.
The small brown lady with huge eyes
imitated Aretha Franklin with verve.
All the counterfeit celebrities
came in costume and annual humor.
Providence poured out to sing out
against its own drab continence.
You watched me make faint
efforts at the dance, try to overcome
my childhood fear of being watched.
I gulped down drink after drink,
but was still sober enough to sense
you were not having a good time,
that you expected more of me.
Perhaps you wanted me to kiss you,
but you certainly wanted more from me
than this pretension with friends—
Lorraine, who could have been Bessie Smith,
Peggy, who could have been Diana Ross,
Claude, who could have been Sammy Davis, Jr.
We all stepped out of ourselves
to forget for a night the borders
of lives too big for the small space
of a city long overdue for acclaim.
I felt a sudden pause in the dance.
I looked at you in your solemnity
with the dress you picked carefully
for this night with me. Your eyes
were not remorse enough to make me
forget the mistake of ever believing you.

Providence Journal IV:
Partying at Peggy's

Barbecued chicken slumbered
in sauce thick and spicy sweet
on the stove. Soft rolls were
nearby. Potato salad
humped its lumps together
in a blue bowl in the refrigerator.
The beer sweated in ice.

We did the limbo dance
in the living room. We rocked
to music that had nothing
to do with limbo. You shook
and rolled like spaghetti,
a woman nimble as a noodle.

And you looked back at me
with a laugh that dared. You
bristled all over like electricity
itself. You asked me to come
in, to come to you, to come
so you could touch me and let go
all the strings that held me,
like the cooked to the raw.

Providence Journal V:
Israel of Puerto Rico

In the clutter and clatter of the Bronx,
your uncle's Chihuahuas tipped
over the tile floors with a song that ticked
with a rhythm like the swirl of the calabash.
You counted the day's wages from the track,
bounced your head like hands above congas.
You popped a rhythm into the living room
where the dominant music was the World Series
on the television where your uncle cheered.

At home in Humacao, your mother gave her sermon
on the dangers of Manhattan, the other island.
There women can turn a good boy like you
into the aching salsa of empty pockets,
hearts chopped down to lifeless fibers.
You nodded your head and promised to obey—
yes to your mother's wisdom, yes to her fear.
In New York your eyes turned at once
to a dance no one can see, the dance of hedonism
wrapped in care, wrapped in a mother's eye
as miraculous and far-ranging as the sun itself.

On Sunday nights we rode back to Providence.
You patted the dashboard and cried out to me,
cried out to the night that snickered outside,
"New York is sweet irony. New York is my poem."

Providence Journal VI:
Celebrating the Play

for George H. Bass

At Cecilia's we had red beans and rice.
We awakened the cook on the bar stool
long after the kitchen had been closed,
the food put away like lonely songs,
only half consumed. We started building
a pile of memories on the table,
laughed about how rehearsal succeeded
and how it failed, and how something
so alive depends on imaginations that
cooperate and synchronize whenever
summoned. When the food came we ate
with good cheer and paper napkins.

I thought that we could return years later
and stir the ashes of this vital magic
that escapes names like a flying ghost.
I did not accept that we will all exit
in our separate ways in unpredictable time.
I did not believe memories and time
were all we had before or after the play.

Providence Journal VII:
Ascensions and Disruptions

for George H. Bass

Think of the outrageous,
of Hughes and Nugent barefoot,
as they stride along through Harlem,
of Hurston as she roars around
the forbidden trope—nigger—
of the way children's games
order our disrupted universe.
Think of calamity as you sing
Shoo, turkey, shoo, a child's refrain.

Think of the intractable,
of the guessing game of abstraction.
Twist a Rhode Island sunrise
into a morning yawn in Nashville,
and paint it with a baptism for art
on a cruise in southern Europe.
Think of the way art begins,
on a single point or in the sum
of a given frame that comes
to sight, sound, touch, taste, smell.
Think of it. Think of nightfall.
It comes early as you glide across
the green in deep, seething reflection.

Think of the infinite recognitions,
how time and drama release us when we die.

Rogan Josh

for Gregory Russell

Our first Indian restaurant
is the one Gregory revealed.
When you saw the delight crawl
into my face you had to have the recipe.
That is how men are secured
in the southern world of your mother,
the world where steaming dishes
of clean, healthy food spell home
to a father, spell love
to a husband. Good food guarantees
the soft security of lives joined
at the marrow, where blood infuses
blood, where breath connects.

Back in Gregory's apartment I played
with Sugar Bear, the laziest chow chow
this side of China. You cut
and seasoned our first rogan josh
concocted outside of the safe mystery
of the restaurant. I played
with Sugar Bear, running my hands
through her black mane, while her nose
showed an appetite that inspires
madness and barking, the uncouth
way men rush to their dinner tables.

Outside, Harlem did its Sunday spin,
a slower movement from the
hurried boogaloo of weekdays
where even the idle foot has a plan,

and some stomachs go empty for days.
Harlem did its holy day festival
of families walking back from church
with little girls skipping and
lifting their plaits with ribbons
and barrettes that shone and clapped,
with mothers waddling back thinking
of the waiting pots and stove,
of the normal hunger of their families,
the hunger that did not threaten life.

In this little apartment with its art,
we recreated the India we knew
down in the East Village, the India
surrounded by New York's commodious
clutter. New York's knickknack elitism is
bound by the crowded cardboard city
of the homeless who live underground.
We sat and chewed the morsels
of your success as I studied the sculpture
from a hungry Africa that stood
and sat like mournful saints
on the speakers, on the walls,
on these shelves in a tiny space,
in the hungry heart of Harlem.

Brooklyn

for Mizan Kirby Nunes

Over Manhattan Bridge,
I land in the breast of Brooklyn,
in the thoroughfares that slap
the earth like fresh switches
in the playful hands of children.
Once in Brooklyn I walked
with Charles, my gossip partner,
through the West Indian festival,
commenting on the floats,
watching Spike Lee sign autographs.
We saw Brooklyn raw,
stepping out of its clothes,
walking toward some conjugal laughter,
its various parts rolling, shaking
in this marvelous vanity parading.

And for my thirty-ninth birthday,
I saw a South African musical
at the Brooklyn Academy of Music,
whose acronym knocks you out.
The colors were sensational.
My wife laughed, Robert napped,
my musical gift beat itself
into the frenzy of townships
and laws that make cities
the shy strangers to their own history,
make them unsure of themselves
with identity crises that set generations
into the bumbling unraveling
of substantiating a culture's place
in the wavering world,
on the moody map.

In my father's sister's home
on the other side of Prospect Park,
I listened to tongues that flow
like bourbon, tongues that
were born in the flat perspective
of Virginia. There the trees rise
like those in a child's drawing,
the scrawling crayon signifying
the need to move up North,
to migrate, to go until something inward
sets your heart to ringing out
a shout. In my aunt's home
on Maple Street, I heard the sputter
of black souls that found Brooklyn
when the Tenderloin fell
into the conquering coffers
of greed. In Brooklyn I saw bare feet circling
in the sand and heard voices singing *home*.

Pearl Bailey

an elegy

Last night the corner of my new shoes
hit the corn I have had since birth.
I let out a silent scream amid
all the polite faces that pretended
their feet never hurt. Not one of them
was as honest as you were when you sat
on the stage, eased the microphone
into your free hand, and took off
those merciless shoes. Those shoes hurt
and tormented old wounds of your feet
like memories that open up heartache.
I thought of how easy you were,
how quick to be like the most ordinary
among us, the unglamorous, the hopeful.
You created your expressions full
of every face we knew in our tired homes,
in our bustling streets, in our hot fields.
You visited the poor and weak.

I reached the corner of the hallway.
I felt ashamed for being so tired and so young.
But I was quite happy to lean on the wall,
and off that painful and mean foot.
I saluted your jazz and your jive.

Sir

for Michael S. Harper

The battle with the bourgeois
is not a matter for lightweights
who do not understand
the bob-and-weave trope,
the stick-and-join rhythm—
Lester Young's problem
with scores and musicologists,
Charlie Christian's inventions
on his electric box,
Billie Holiday's mysterious
lift of melody away from beat,
Coltrane's symphonic
survey of the inner circles,
Jimmy Rushing's smooth blues
that cried out in his face,
Charlie Parker's lessons
from Buster Smith—
all the flatted fifths,
all the dominant sevenths
of black people as they create.

The battle with the bourgeois
is a whisper we shared
on a sidewalk when you
presumed that I understood,
and I did understand.
I named the colors of your words,
looked in your inquisitive eye,
saw an image of myself,
and called you

"Sir."

Destinations:
Saints and Solitude

"The craft of weaving in fact," said Ogotemmêli in conclusion, "is the tomb of resurrection, the marriage bed and the fruitful womb."

It remained only to speak of the Word, on which (he said) the whole revelation of the art of weaving was based.

"The Word," said the old man, "is in the sound of the block and the shuttle. The name of the block means 'creaking of the word.' Everybody understands what is meant by 'the word' in that connection. It is interwoven with the threads; it fills the interstices in the fabric. It belongs to the eight ancestors; the first seven possess it; the seventh is the master of it; it is itself the eighth."

"The weaver," he explained, "sings as he throws the shuttle, and the sound of his voice enters into the warp, adding to and taking along with it the voice of the ancestors. For the weaver is Lébé, the man of the eighth family and consequently the Word itself."

—MARCEL GRIAULE
Conversations with Ogotemmêli

*Don't let nobody fool you.
Not everybody needs to be
   brought down. Some folk
   need to be brought up.*

—DONALD FAULCON

Boston, 1972

We all flirted with the Puerto Rican woman
who had round hips and braided, woolen hair.
She corralled with the other women,
as a lone foreigner. She flipped above the net
of identity, of contention, of escape. She tantalized
those who understood that she was black,
but not the black of American categories.
Her blackness was color that was only incidental
and inconclusive, like the character of shadows.

I remember only parting glances, the smile
that teased as I shot up, drunken and rude,
from my berth in the car. We were headed
for Boston, soldiers on leave from camp.
We cackled and smothered the faces
of discontent in ethnic jokes over the hatred.
Our humor let us live with each other
like a garden overspent with varieties,
each legitimately beautiful but intolerant of beauty.

We split and rushed apart. We separated
in Boston into like groups at the Commons.
The whites headed confidently into Boston proper.
The blacks looked for a nightclub with
the Voices of East Harlem, young singers
who hurtled toward a bright but brief fame.
Boston looked on with eyes raised
in suspicion, the suspicion of aristocracy
and hands as solemn as Cambridge in England.

I listened to the vocalists, thought of America
the insuperable, of how the Spanish woman
would not come into our meaning. We soldiers had

a tough and noble churlishness, a mean handsomeness
that would whisk away a woman like music.
But she would not be wounded or winsome.
At camp she walked past me slowly, rhythmically.
Her lips held down a smile that hinted at
giving my world, my spirit, the gift of a new visa.

Talk Radio from Boston

From the white lights of the radio,
the truthful soul of America came.
It examined, explicated itself,
rubbed the soft belly of America.
A voice of a woman chirped in,
announced the decline of business
in her ice-cream parlor, where
children come to jam their fingers
in the glass that separates them
from the toppings, a display
four feet long with every
rendition of sugar and nut
crushable in the young molars
that grind in anxious and desperate
hunger. In her voice the fatalistic
image of failure arose and cast itself
in front of me, on the road.
I felt sad for someone who can lose
thousands of dollars in a month.
The host reminded her of deductions
to be made on her taxes. I lost
interest, beckoned by the polite
way the night held itself to me.

Another woman lit the airways,
this time about sex and love.
She bemoaned the way men use women,
the bumptious way they decline
to express their motives, their
feelings. He had a woman before her.
This previous woman was a jezebel
still in the antechambers of his heart.
After the initial suspicion that

this jezebel still swayed his thoughts,
there came the proof in his libido.
She felt unmistakably that he
was thinking of the jezebel while
they were in the throes of passion.
"What do I do about my anger,
Mr. Talk Show Host. What do I do
about my dreams where I kill them?"
The host reminded her that
there is a web of weakness inside us.
We need to get to know it,
to trouble its contours with thoughts
that tickle it like curious hands.
Then we know why it is we fall
down the precipice of love,
as love should be instead a stroll
along a plateau. She hung up,
after a lumpy throat thank you.

A man from Baltimore called,
talked about the Orioles,
about the expectant way he sat
and watched and listened as
they lost game after game, with so much
to play with, youth and talent.
The host said, "What is losing
after all, except that we have to
force our egos to sit down and shut up?"
The man from Baltimore held silent
across the breadth of America,
on millions of radios looking to hear
the republic enunciate the song
that fills its facetious garment

of a soul. Then he told the host
the Orioles need a new manager,
that God is the supreme manager,
and He won't come to Baltimore for
less than five million a year.
The host cut him off, and I cut off
the host, lured by a quiet victory.

I sent a hurrah like a lance
into the New England night.
I smiled at the caller from Baltimore,
my home, and meditated on the
company of strangers on the road—
truckers wired to stay up for two days,
late commuters who hobble in from work,
families on vacation from the heat,
lovers who rush to discreet rendezvous,
teenagers who return their parents' cars—
the carnival wonder of a wild nation
that will not admit or see me.

Easy Living

for Dorothy West

From the shiny iron stove,
where your mother cooked,
you move to your small writing table
past the foot-high, yellow dictionary.
You remember the days your mother
took you and your rainbow cousins
out to shock the white folks.
Your mother had a cream color,
her pink cheeks against your gingersnap
brown you call an apolitical colored.

Your mother forbade you to ever
set foot in the South. She told you
about her mother, who was a slave.
This slave grandmother of yours
had eleven children by her master.
One day, a little girl who was your aunt
stepped on the tail of her white father's dog.
Your grandfather went into a rage
and he killed your grandmother's daughter.
The South still frightens you.

Your Oak Bluffs cottage sits
like a dollhouse on Myrtle Avenue.
You see an image arise.
It is your father as he sells
the restaurant in Richmond
that he opened with his mother.
He moved north to Springfield, Massachusetts,
to the produce stand that made him
Boston's black banana king and

allowed him to buy a brick house
on Brookline Avenue and the summer home
on Martha's Vineyard. He ached
to leave you more when he died,
more than the memory of his blue eyes.

Sometimes black but certainly colored,
you reminisce about your news column,
"The Cottager's Corner," where you chronicled
the island's famous colored, like
the first black college president.
Then Wallace Thurman comes to mind,
and you remember with a smile
Langston Hughes, whom you asked in a letter
to marry you—and have children with you.
You think of how he declined the offer,
and you look out the window and chuckle.
On the island there is no time for regrets.
You serve your tenure gracefully,
evidence of a world with wonders
like your small hand in Langston's
in the cold Atlantic, churning to a Russian film,
to the eye that makes the memory.

Swimming Near Mt. Washington

for Kala Oboi

As we chew the brown bread,
we shuffle down the gravel road.
It slopes so quickly, so abruptly
we have to rock back on our heels.
We grumble to think of walking back
up a hill so merciless it laughs.
The sun spills into the foliage,
makes pavilions of light that mix
the solar yellow with leaves and bark.

At the pond New Hampshire's natives
are here with their babies
in disposable diapers and shirts.
Their mothers smoke while fathers
ease the babies in and out
in mock baptisms with prayers of giggles.
The children's tiny mouths pop open
like fish who nibble at the surface.

We stride in heavily.
Father and son, two mountains,
we are the blackest beings on the beach.
We part the water with our stone edges.
Our rumps gleam as our flesh
revels in its fullness and heaviness.
The fish and the natives
give us more room than we need,
smile with hesitation and anxiety.

We head out for a swim,
slip into the surprise of an eddy.

The Nameless Lake

for Aissatou Mijiza

We changed in your wooden house
where you lived with women artists
and old chairs and magazines
and thoughts of what to see,
what revelations for the eye.
In the wooden house you thought
of what to create for the touch,
what worlds lay within the world.
You thought of what could rival
nature with its tactfulness,
with its excess. Dressed for the lake,
we dropped our trappings
on the grass shore near the rocks,
the Sunday *New York Times*.

We touched the cold water.
You laughed a four-year-old laugh
like the snapshot I keep of you.
Slipping on the rocks, we sat
and edged into the lake like geriatrics,
afraid of breaking what won't mend.
We could feel the rubber bottom
of the lake under our feet.
We wiped algae from our hands
and discovered hidden transmission
centers where Earth talks with
worlds locked away in constellations.
Along the edge of the lake,
we watched the trees in slumped
salutations to the power boat
and the seaplane landing.

We had waded in front of the wooden house
where men artists lived with their
sketches of the uncreated. Our friends
sat on a floating platform and called
out to us to swim over, but I held you
close and cautioned you against
tiring and falling victim to the lake.
I sailed you in an inner tube
along the edge and fondled you
under the water where innocence
is still wild-eyed and naive.

Chris's milky white body
rose like a slow missile
from the water as we laughed
at our friends who sneered
while we avoided them.
Chris climbed to the grass
near the paper and cheered
while we let love loose
in the lake around our wish
to be naked and uncontained,
like unabashed lovers reveling
before the loon's deliverance,
before I left in the afternoon.
Driving away, I held to
the black blue of the water,
the clap of its laughter
on the rocks, the contentment
that clothed and protected you.

The Final Trains of August

for Michael S. Harper

He stands in the unfinished door
of his antique shop, above Bar Harbor.
He leans on the sill to relieve
his trick knees, watches
the final trains of August,
vacationers with their bicycles
on the tops of r.v.'s and minivans,
teenagers with their feet propped
in the window. They mimic
some abandon coined a long way off.
He counts the possible customers,
the accountants from Boston
with their neat wives who move
through his collection smug and sure,
like necromancers who make money
out of the sagacious purchase,
or the infrequent southerners
who betray summers of the South
for the cool nights and mountains
of Maine with its wilderness
and its infinite lay of lakes.
He watches and imagines
what stragglers will land
in his world of sundry history.

"I want a window," she says,
and Walter announces himself.
He holds out his pearl white beard,
"Walter Francis, retired colonel
and antique trader at your service."
"I want a window," she repeats.

He takes her into the basement,
past some yellow Jehovah's Witness
books spread in a basket,
past the collection of chairs
where people had their breakfast
or where they watched the chill
of autumn come in with full colors.
They move past tables where folks served tea
to neighbors who passed time with grace,
past the baby scale where doctors
held protesting children to see
how much they had grown back
before the electronic scale and Similac.
They reach the old windows.
Her face breaks open and brightens.
"Where is this from, what time,
what house?" She presses her palm to a pane.
"Ma'am, I get these windows
from all over this region and beyond."
She persists, prodding on,
"What house, what house is this?"
He pulls the suspenders holding him,
"Ma'am, this was a quiet house,
off to itself, where the rain
beat like light fingers on a drum."
She takes it quickly, writes
the check in tight, even letters,
announces that she is an artist.
Walter lights a Marlboro.
"I get them all," he muses,
"everybody comes to Walter Francis."

"Gertrude and I built this place,"
he tells a couple from Hartford.

Gertrude walks across the road.
"She runs the motel, and I run
this fabulous collection of the old."
Gertrude reaches them, moves
as easy as a teenager with legs
long and supple as they were
when she was an Air Force lieutenant
to Walter's Vietnam colonel.
They believed that nothing
but the end could stop them,
the end that comes to all of us,
and to everything we own,
the end that falls to the care in
hands of angels and preservationists.
She reaches them, speaks loudly,
"Walter, I'm gonna unload that truck.
It'll be dark soon, too dark to work."
He growls softly, "Gertrude
get on back to the motel. Go on."
She ignores him, moves to the truck, tosses
in the new antiques like a stevedore,
things new to this way station
of the old but unforgotten.
"That woman thinks she's my boss,
after I took this business
to be rid of the overseers, the judges."
The young couple ponder
a relay box from the 1880s,
precisely kept in a wooden cabinet
polished, tightened, and smoothed.
They decline and move out
into the brisk air of the evening,
to make the night drive to Hartford.

The last stranger fills the threshold,
a young man who travels alone. He is
up from Providence to see the mountain
of the Roosevelts, Cadillac Mountain,
where F.D.R. came to forget
the weight of guiding America.
The stranger considers
buying an old-fashioned life preserver
made of tamarack wood.
Walter takes his cue to land
a lecture on the origin of his house,
built in the eighteenth century
by a man who built frigates and schooners
for a living. Walter explains the house
is a seagoing vessel, tight and solid.
He could lift it and move it
today and not even disturb it.
The nursery floor is tamarack
because that kept life's noise at bay.
The house has outlived endings.
The stranger pushes his fingers
into the night air, marvels
at the stars. Walter reminisces
about the Orient where he wondered
if adventure lay in what the dead
leave behind. In the sick humidity
of Vietnam, he made a regular route
to our last heralded door and stopped
just short of hearing the answers.
The stranger from Providence
coughs to break the meditation
and then climbs roughly into
an old Chevrolet with scabs of rust.
He drives away toward the ocean.

Walter hobbles on his trick knees,
turns off the lights, closes down
the shop with its unfinished walls.
At the road's edge, he lights a Marlboro,
blows the smoke ahead, walks into it,
as he listens to the regrets of the dead.

In C. W.'s Closet

I climb the C scale on the old piano.
On the third finger, I forget
the crossover step like a man forgets
a kiss. You chuckle, rupture
the stillness of Indian Pond, hustle
over to the window, look out over
the blueberry field you knew as a child.
Then you turn gracefully as someone
sixty years younger with the gray hair
blonde, the brittle frame full
with flesh. You turn and beckon me
to your closet, to the past.

In the personal closet your father stands
in photographs where you toddle along,
you and Elizabeth at the end
of the Gilded Age. She has her gumption,
you your willingness to obey
the root of the law over our tainted bodies,
the blossom of the law over our souls.
Your father stands in his rebuke
of DuBois, the black rabble rouser,
after the Niagara Falls convention.
Disparate fingers were called together,
before I settled into your domain,
a heavy bird with inchoate wings.

You pull back and sigh, eye me
with the deadlock desperation we sing
when we know the flower must wither,
the stone must crumble, the friend must go.
We unlock from our fixed gaze
on your father in his belief
in segregation. We move together

into the kitchen, young and old,
black and white, poor and rich.
Our bodies are so close they pattern a rhythm
above the evening news with Tom Brokaw,
above the world as it wanes, moans.
Our breath mingles with the night.

Going to Church with C. W.

We spellbind like the annunciation.
You amble over to your cane,
favor the leg that threatens to surrender.
I shuffle over to the cordless phone
to peek at the red recharging indicator.
Two cantankerous supplicants, we head
for a New England church, wooden and white,
an eightyish white woman with her companion,
a thirtyish black man with his diva.
We slip through the wet grass to worship.

Down the road, Jesus. Down the road to joy.
Shadows of the congregations of leaves
whip over the car like a lover's whine.
You ask me about the book I manage
barely to write, slowly, with pain.
You resurrect again your Radcliffe degree
in literature, your fondness for Victorian fiction.
I remind you of your rude impertinence,
how worship blurts out our duty
to be meditative, to acknowledge the splendor
of the sun's confident slide over the mountains,
of the minute splash of butterflies in the stream.

I come Lord, come this way to please you.
We waddle into the temple. Floors creak,
heads turn, eyes spin, and mouths drop
as we go to the front pew. You fix
your eyes on your almost century of life,
from the roads, the dirt roads before the car
to the unmarked highway that leads to the moon.
I wonder how long I can stay in your grace,
how the separation will wake one sad day,
how we will find excuses to hurt each other.

Through the benediction and the hush,
we walk together outside, an unusual machine
turning on the pistons of forgiveness and curiosity.
Halfway home we stop at a store for ice cream.
You blink quickly over the dashboard.
I pay for our diversion. The clouds
suggest a thunder far away and above us
like the noise from flesh's integration
as our hearts circle one another and join.
The wind sticks wet lips to us as we drive home
to the squeak and creak of the colonial farmhouse,
up the winding path along the stone wall.
Hold my hand, Father. Hold my hand when I die.

The Spanish Lesson

for Jay Wright

It is late, and I hurry
up to Seventeenth Street
from the PATH station
facing a roasted nut stand.
Police on the corners
smile in pressed uniforms,
patrolling wooden barricades
while Sixth Avenue
lies open like a black ribbon
to the dense skyscrapers
in midtown that crowd
the sky wincing above.
I realize slowly
that a parade is coming with
the proud, red antique
engines of the fire companies
from an America
of more secure boundaries,
of defensible difference,
of ethnic occupations.

Moving past them,
wading through their era,
I ring the bell
of Blackburn's Printmaking Workshop,
something else that
will crowd history's ears.
Aisha, recently from India,
opens the door, and I tread
up the stairs to my lessons
in *la lengua and la cultura* of Mexico,

and Carmen smiles from the light
of the window near Sixth Avenue.
We talk about *los conquistadores,*
as we begin our lesson with lunch,
and I mention my Puerto Rican
hermanito from Humacao,
how we adopted each other
in cold rains in Providence.
I remember my little brother
as I think of Hughes
showing Guillén the Cuban *son,*
of Guillén showing Hughes
the universe beyond color.

Carmen says we have had enough
of this garrulous gluttony,
so we tackle simple tenses,
she testing me in clear Spanish
as I struggle with a brain
twenty-five years older
than the one that learned
French in 1963,
after King's march on the capital.
My French teacher shot
the questions at us, and
I fired them back
so that even now
France has a lover's seduction
that I learned in Baltimore,
the city of common sense
and very little Spanish.

We go from the tenses
to conversation, and she gives me

a magazine from Mexico,
one I can manage to read,
to build my vocabulary.
We take a break from it
for sodas, coming back to chatter
more and more in a *lengua*
hearkening back to Madrid,
to the kind clerk there
who reminded me sternly
to guard against thieves
on the long walks
down to where I could see
the mountains on the horizon
and eat *helado*.
We chatter and she teaches me
the tone of Spanish,
much like the woman,
a classical pianist,
who taught me Chinese
on Sunday afternoons
in an antechamber of a Lutheran church,
where all seven of us
chirped like newborn chicks
at the characters she drew
on the board precisely,
teaching us the order
of right to left,
downward and outside in.
I thought ponderously of
what the Cantos might have been
had Pound learned Chinese
phonetically, had he sung
an alphabet song

in a language which has
no alphabet, had he sung it
in a church basement
to a captive audience
on Chinese New Year's,
while polite mothers
smiled and his teacher
kept him sternly inside
the five tones with a grimace.

We end the lesson,
a day of Spanish and eating.
The parade is gone,
the street back to business.
We walk prudently
through beggars and chic women,
not wanting to let go
of the union that appears
when lives cross through
the languages of their birth,
and we linger on the corner
not far from Union Square,
then part, disappearing
down separate subway entrances.

I catch the eye
of a beggar, black as I am
and singing old and rough,
the way the blues ache,
as his poverty and pity
hurtle me back into history.
I think for one second
of tongue beside unknowing tongue

in crowded holds
that affirm for one moment
my son's African name,
its prophetic certainty.
In the belly of the city,
I lean against a column,
waiting for the hollow rattle
of the train, listen
to the chatter of black Latinas
with their children, and
I fall into the echolalia
of Spanish children eating shish kebab,
their mothers conjugating *amar,*
white women singing to Walkmans,
and the duty to love
knock, knock, knocking
through our hearts
as the spirits spill
from mouths of strangers.

Hamilton Place

for Gregory Russell

Down the spiral hallway
with its concrete and elevator
that smells like old piss,
I walk onto Hamilton Place,
which runs alongside Amsterdam Avenue.
The conga drums resonate from
the car speakers as deep as wells,
popping until the fenders are drums
that push in and out, moved by
the giant hands of percussion.

At the first corner, the gesture
and the smile beckon me, entice me
to buy drugs from eyes cracked
by sleeping late in the afternoon,
Dealers ignore the verisimilitude
of proverbs from fathers and mothers,
the etchings on city walls.
I escape the first nefarious clocker
and make the turn down to Broadway,
to the tattered colors of bodegas
and Spanish restaurants. I marvel
at the way the sun lies just ahead,
at the end of this block where
life hangs haggard in the twelfth round.
I see the floating prayers of the old
sift above me into the welcoming sky.

The festival of Broadway overtakes me.
I stand near fruit in the sun,
looking at the rush of life.

A final drug salesman peeps from a shadow
in the corner I have just left, like
a vampire afraid of the sun's divinity,
of its power woven with the cross.
And on the sidewalk with my foot,
I pat out the names of the canonized—
this is where Hughes sang Harlem's patois,
this is where Ellington scored Harlem's hymns,
this is where Bearden envisioned Harlem's soul.
The light changes, I head for fast food.
I remember that I must get back to work,
to my thinking by the window open
to the business of the street, dreaming
of what to create while noise of people
wondering what it is to live cavorts
just under my chin, inside this world
legislated by need, vindicated by art.

Harlem Dreams:
The Chosen City, the Chosen
People

By 1920 Afro-American expansion in Harlem no longer depended entirely upon sharp realtors and their mulatto and white front men. . . . East of Eighth to the Harlem River, from 130th to 145th streets, lay black Harlem, the largest, most exciting urban community in Afro-America or anywhere else, for that matter. . . . Harlem had seemed to flash into being like a nova. The war ended, and there it was, with its amalgam of money and misery, values and vices, hope and futility.

—David Levering Lewis
When Harlem Was in Vogue

Music is my mistress.

—Duke Ellington

Harlem Society

for Gwendolyn Brooks

We have split the silk and satin air
of the evening with rough laughter and gay
gestures. Around the glasses of fair
liaisons of vermouth and gin we play.
Vertiginous romances engage, pair
heart with heart in abandon's display.

We wear flowers in our hair to beguile
the night. It pulls its colossal cloak
around us like some mastodon, a mile
thick in its envious heart. The smoke
of its infinite body courts the smile
of pastel glass. We make a brave joke.

We forget the pardons, innocence
we fight for against the hopelessness
of being who we are. This is our sense.
Natural laws forgive and hide the mess
of enmity, lock it behind a fence
high and invisible, mock kindness.

Our gentle men meet our eyes with the hope
that the porous soul of jealous night
will hold itself there forever. The slope
of our sleekness in our dresses is as light
as the first breath or kiss. The tropes
of the men's eyes follow, keen and slight.

Our loquacity thickens the space.
We start, move like one linked body,
held by the union of the party's pace

to a universe glamorous, not shoddy.
Enticed, we celebrate with a sublime grace
that hangs on our collective body.

We hold our cigarettes in our thin hands.
Our bosoms heave with elegance. Anxious
to catch every gesture in the grand
portrait we pour onto memory, a fatuous
hate hangs outside, dares us to understand
its intent. We crown ourselves *marvelous*.

Parade

for George Mayo

Our army in its finery
steps, courses the avenue.
It wears the infinite frivolity,
tassels in white, sashes in blue.
With infectious hilarity,
hats off, heads up, pride preens thru.

With the flash, dash of mock sabers,
a whole river halts for solos.
Music pierces the staid onlookers.
The whole river deepens. Heroes
rise from regalia. Marchers
knead a culture with its woes.

Open the windows. Celebrate.
Throw on your hat. Fall in the crowd.
Let the pots simmer. Congregate.
Meet the marchers, glorious, loud.
Come into the swell. Vacate
despair, angst. Join the proud.

Street Orator

for Lucille Clifton

Impresario in cameos,
maestro of the polished fine,
immaculate inamoratas are mine.
I seek to sleekly and lavishly bestow
approbation on my portfolio.
I have curls, bosoms, sumptuous lines,
manifestations of passion and fine
romance in mansions. My dreams are aglow

with ladies languishing in Raleigh.
They sigh in tangled silk dresses abloom.
Breathless, they fume over my profligate hive

in Harlem. They mourn and inveigh
and wait. Magnificent, over all, I loom
aplomb, mordant—the master of jive.

Pool Parlor

for Gwendolyn Brooks

All the cats and their sensibilities.
Eager hands ease, thumbs itch and play
off electric blood. Dudes' eyes key
off the unsure bet and steady clay.
Balls battle for mouths that see
hope hang with a whole week's pay.
They shout through the cigarette smoke,
"Come on baby, don't leave me broke."

A stranger comes in, walks a little heavy
for a hustler. He pushes down the volume
with each meditated fall of his foot to see
how the tongues and lips fail. He exhumes
the fear buried with their shallow security
in their plebeian talents. Their glee
escapes them now as he pulls out
a customized stick and moves about.

Wads of rent money and grocery money cling
to cotton pockets like mice who evade the paws
of a hungry tabby. The fear stings.
The eyes and throats clog as single flaws
appear. Someone has a weak bank shot, flings
the ball to the left. Another has a caw
like a crow on the scratch. Assured of ten
games at least, the young lord counts the men.

A boy not long from Alabama steps up.
He's a skinny cat who has a wife who rejects few.
Everybody keeps quiet about it so this pup
won't go crazy and level Harlem, undo
himself and every soul he can cup

his hands against. No one wants to skew
his image of his wife's fidelity. Here
now, he is shamefully brave and austere.

The young lord lays the plan.
It is a simple game of eight ball, no
complications that will unwind this man
from Alabama too soon. Slow
humiliation hovers. The ceiling fan
hums above the stillness. This is a clan
of men wedded by social rites
of corners rife with gin and knife fights.

The table full of his balls, Alabama
chokes and stokes his fire. The ace
from nowhere has hands that urge Alabama's
mama's admonition. Indignation's face
pushes Alabama's rage into the penumbra
of wiped brows and worried lips that pace.
They all wonder who will get it first.
It breaks. Alabama's fire bursts.

Above the sensibilities, key notes run.
The combo plays. Hearts beat hearts.
It's a hip and down game boys should shun.

Jukebox, 1946

for Gregory Russell

When the jukebox came to Richmond,
Nellie was seventeen in bare feet and plaits.
She watched in Mabel's window as rotund
women danced to a sage and silent éclat.

She itched over the bits of sand, babbled
in her house. She danced to unheard music.
Outside her window were tiny eyes of rabble,
boys who begged, arched their eyes, bucolic.

Now in Harlem, Nellie is an empty dress
that spins in the infinite pool of a memory.
She rushes for the jukebox to bless
her, like an altar, with sensuous glory.

Come on girl and cut that step. Swing.
The stupor of loneliness and liquor
kill the persistent pain and sting.
She leans on the jukebox made for her.

In the blur and swirl, she is placated
by the intoxication of her hope.
She clings to a space others vacated.
Come on girl and cut that step. Swing.

Bootleg Whiskey
for Twenty-five Cents

for Jaye T. Stewart

They lap up their liquor with virtuosity,
the stiff imports from Macon, Georgia,
the velvet brand from Memphis, Tennessee,
the West Indian cool from Florida.
They sway together upstairs at Jackie's.
They listen to Duke on the radio. Codas
coddle the heads on necks of putty
that taste jazz with home brew and sodas.

Their new shoes are from downtown
with Italy stamped inside. Their dresses
came to them from full closets where a frown
from wealth shines down. The city confesses
to ballrooms where corn liquor is thrown down
like New York water. A few undress,
love. They can't do better or worse. The gown
of gaiety envelops them, possesses.

They debate the undebatable. They drift away,
in Jackie's back room, in syncopated sway.

Funeral Sermon, 1946

As we leave the space of grief awhile,
our Esther reminds me of a profile
of another Esther. This girl, this Hadassah,
was raised by her Uncle Mordecai in Susa,
when Jews lived under King Ahaseurus.
He was a king who let mischief abide. With us
now are leaders who turn away,
who turn their eyes when they betray
us. There was Esther, a young woman
with a chaste heart, a woman's
courage, who became queen of Persia,
flying into history's mania.
In pride and fear, Mordecai paced the courtyard
each evening, prayed Esther could replace hard
and silly Queen Vashti like a river
that swells with its currents fuller
than banks that hold it and oppress
its rush and foam. It is a roar that can bless
and make new geography, *children.*
I say new geography is forged by women
like our own Esther who lies here asleep.
Our Esther ministered and had to weep.
Esther of old wept after Mordecai
told her Haman set it so Jews would die
from India to Ethiopia, young and old.
Esther listened and slowly grew bold,
afraid of Ahaseurus's sacred edict—
uninvited folks in his room would inflict
death upon themselves. No one entered
his apartment unless he conferred
permission to visit. What a woman
she was because she did what a woman
will do without due credit. She will reach

down in her soul for courage and teach
the strongest man in here about
what life can do to make you shout.
What a woman, this Esther,
like our Esther before us. Our Esther
also had messengers come to her
like Hathach who revealed how further
efforts were needed. Among us she rose
in Harlem's old streets and chose
life over death just like Esther of old
who is nowhere in history I am told
except in this Old Testament book.
This book of Purim, of victory, is Esther's book.
She saved the Jews, became queen as she took
history by the neck, grabbed it, shook
until the situation was in her favor.
The king and Haman found the flavor
of her feasts irresistible and returned
until Ahaseurus said, "You have served
me well, prepared a luscious feast.
What you would have I would grant." The beast
that threatened the Jewish people found
his plans unraveled as the soft sound
of Esther's voice asked for the lives sung
by an entire nation. She had Haman hung
on gallows he built for her dear uncle.
Mordecai would not prostrate, buckle
down before humans. Esther saved the race,
children. Yes, she did. Her face was like the face
looking solemn, peaceful, right under
this pulpit a few thousand years later.
Our saint escaped the plots set around her.

Beloved Esther, our sweet, brave Esther.

Masks

Masks undress,
go naked. They ask,
"Who will bless
the sardonic task?"

Who will kill
the grin and lie?
Who will fill
truth's empty eye?

Masks in motion
lift and fly
the question—
Who am I?

Village Quartet

for George Mayo

Four gentlemen in sable at the Vanguard
sit in red jackets. Smooth explosions
of notes set minute dance motions
to dangle in heads that dip, hang hard
on the revelations of the blue note.
Their jazz and blues are sassy inventions
by unlettered hands. The smooth tensions
are marked *genuine* by a composer's vote.

The soprano sax taunts the guitar,
sets its fast mouth to a grim stance.
The trumpet tramples the countenance
of the trombone whose nose goes afar.
It investigates silence's edge, the tar
river between them and the audience.
The four sable gentlemen's experience
works keys, reeds, class—bar by bar.

Rock Skippin' at the Blue Note

for Abena Joan Brown

Outside the club, before I walked in,
a humble old man with a saxophone
lifted his ax upward above the din.
Footsteps and chatter shone
like the billion silvery faces of sophistry
that organize into superb choirs.
When I am rattling across country
on the train, the imperturbable fires
of sleep are held down by my single
wish to strike at the porous heart
of composition. The perfect sound, ample
and resolute, is no larger than any part
of a singular life. Passersby dropped
quarters and sometimes dollars in his hat.
They smiled, sank into sympathy, plopped
down beside all impossible melody, sat
for a commiserating moment, quietly.
Every musician who has ever wanted
to go past sound to silence superbly,
who has ever wanted to be invited
back to the beginning of this world's time
to beat undersides of heaven succinctly
and take the treasure of being sublime,
has risked tragedy with grandiosity.
Through the smoke of my cigarette
I saw the old man was gone. He waddled
through the crowd with his change. Set
in the last summation, he transcended,
while I skipped rocks at the Blue Note.

Willie "the Lion" Smith

for Amiri Baraka

Some unaware, wet-behind-the-ear
types would come in and see Willie.
He sat at the piano with this clear,
still look in his eye, deliberately
chomped on his cigar. He eyed
the way they walked, their pride.

And they would ask him real
carefully if they could play something.
He would say, "What you feel
like, kid?" Or he would pick something
and invite them to sit down
at the Lion's piano and get on down.

Then he would pick 'em apart.
"Where did you break your left hand?"
They would falter, their art
still too far from Willie's stand.
He would remind them with shows
of his prowess—"This is how that goes!"

Dancers

Chick Webb and Billy Strayhorn
moved inside our heads with sound.
They danced with shoes that hit around
invisible points where rhythm is born.

Or they moved like rotund ladies.
A delayed bounce, swish, and sway
rocked you into a melody the way
grand movement entices, empties.

Inside their world of pitch and tone,
Of vibrato and rhythm, figures danced.
These thoughts were immaculate, entranced
bodies with crystal eyes, ivory bone.

So even if they stopped, stood still,
before the band, inside their universe
they danced a choreography in verse.
They gave us movement only spirit can feel.

Billy Strayhorn

When genius strolls, graces in,
fills your life, it is usually
unexpected, like a big win
at a gambler's table. You weakly
look fortune in its own grin,
and, if truly lucky, see the future.

Billy came like this, from the gate
of his own superb talent.
He looked into the scat of fate.
He gave my music a heaven-sent
permanence. It still resonates
wherever people long for *the sound*.

I left him at 381 Edgecombe,
up on Sugar Hill, and went to Europe.
He went to work, combed
through my scores to develop
orchestrations that would become
standards. He adorned the face of jazz.

Sidney Bechet

No one could ever *call* the way
Bechet did. He squeezed that soprano sax
so that a vision from our own lax
recollections poured forth in a display.

We all tried to call back then.
We summoned like *meisters* the private
moments curled up inside ultimate,
forgotten corners of us, tucked, hidden.

While Bubber Miley cut him,
Bechet would step backstage to drink.
He yelled out who he was gonna think
to call next, what soul, what whim.

The people sitting at their tables
didn't know that he was a conjurer.
He told tales by making murals stir
with messages that hung like a jazz fable.

We were in our own dimension,
as we made a deliberate suspension.

Duke Ellington Remembers
Josephine Baker

The city holds to certain types,
to the raucous, the emboldened,
to those who exude the ripe
posture of high society. Addicted,
the city must have these types
to have its glamour brightened.

With Josephine Baker it got
more than a Versailles ball.
She had a splendor and audacity not
in the French memory hall.
Josephine was as grand as the lot
of surprises on a Dali wall.

She blew away the Paris fake
chic when she came. A chorus girl
determined to be famous, she made
the city's lure fresh in a genuine whirl.
Naked, exquisite, she fades
into *Shuffle Along* as a chorus girl.

I had many friends who stayed.
They made this city of love
their home. None of them made
Paris so dizzy, played above
its ache to retrieve an old parade.
No one could top this *Chocolate Kiddie*.

Chicago

for Abena Joan Brown

When we drove up to the lake shore,
I got out of the car and stood,
looked over Lake Michigan. The chore
of unpacking done, I thought I could
take in the city I heard talked
about so much by Pullman porters.
When I was just a boy, they walked
around like well-heeled travelers.
As I listened to the cadence
of the water's slide over itself,
I wondered what superlative sense
my father would make as he felt himself
becoming poetic at a scene
like this. In this aristocrat
of a city where negroes could lean
on wealth's immaculate tract,
what would my father say?
Then I got back into the car.
We rolled through the heft gray
of dusk back to the hotel bar
where two unsavory types waited
for me, two thugs from the underside
of the city. They truly expected
me to be threatened and ride
out of town. They wanted me to pay up.
I quickly called a friend. He called
a friend until the chain reached up
to the top where power was installed.
Al Capone gave the adamant message
that guaranteed my safety

in this magnificent assemblage
of opulence and violence. In this city
I moved to ponder once again
America's profligacy, its sinful gain.

New York

for Mizan Kirby Nunes

After all the pat clichés,
the common pronouncements,
it's still a city where it pays
to be seen. Any achievements
done here will reverberate
around the globe amazingly.
Nowhere else will ever rate
with this city. Opulently
bestowed with raw, open power,
they take the poor dreams
and shoot the breath, empower
it with life until it beams
supremely. Alongside silver spoons
in the mouths of the natural
rich, those whose grand boons
were given, along with cultural
graces, at birth, in this city
anyone can be anyone.
When the courage dims low,
even then you'll see someone
still "putting on" a show.
They stride like a million dollars,
but without two pennies to rub
together. Their suits holler
when pressed. Amid the hubbub
of one of the few places
where I have walked along
in early morning, the faces
inside the bulging throng
after a late-night gig

made me feel that I was in
my own bejeweled, big
palace. There my hopes, thin
and beyond me, suddenly
burst into body and being.
I could feel absolutely
rich, and though tired, reeling
from playing all night, I slowly
counted my wealth. I was drunk
on the splendor, cosmopolitan
par excellence of this hunk
of concrete and steel. Quotidian
yet marvelous, here every thread
of every culture is wound
into a braided fabric spread
over an inviting ground,
an island called Manhattan.

Blues in Orbit

for Amiri Baraka

Busted from dollars to pennies,
broke beyond broke, he moved his keys
in his pocket to get the sound
of metal as it jangled around.
He awoke just five minutes
before his stop, his penance
about to begin. He looked
at his bass in its case, hooked
safely inside. Something tore
away deep in his flesh, an old sore
reopened. He swallowed
and pulled back from the hallowed
pit of regret, almost remembered
how his father ranted, countered,
slammed the door in his young face.
He forgot his usual grace
and said an A.M.E. minister
should have a doctor for a son, better
that than some junky musician.
Held there, he remembered the fustian
stance of his preacher father,
as the train pulled him closer
to home, and finally to the platform.
He thought he saw her form
for a minute, then he recalled
she would never be called
a bitch in public. He found a cabby,
an old friend who was unlucky,
too, but willing to drive him home
with the meter off like in Rome.
There one night he lost his wallet

and got into a cab, his jacket
stinking of wine, and fell asleep.
He woke to find himself in a heap
on his own bed, the driver having
pitied another musician.
Then he was home. The physician
of his father's dreams would likely
have flown in and driven a Caddy.
His wife started in on him
right away, drove him into the dim
lit chair by the open window.
He could see the yellow glow
of the bar sign in the night air.
He caught the mischievous stare
of a pretty woman, fresh and young,
who stepped from the bar where she hung
out with failed saxophonists
and pianists who never made the lists.
His wife beat on, made him
wince as she screamed, high and grim,
from the kitchen. He wondered
when it was that she ever lured
him into loving her, how he could
account for the way she stood
now robbed of any semblance
of beauty. He wished the parlance
of young bodies fevered with desire
would come back, but the only fire
was in his bass case, with the shape
that mocked a woman. Her nape
fell back against him as he
walked up behind her and she
allowed him to embrace her,

run his fingers up and down her
belly. That night they ate quietly
and, in bed, he moved to slowly
undo her gown. She scolded
him like an irritated snake folded
up for its retreat from a beat life.
He rolled over and felt his life
like a dollar rumpled until
you can't see the designs that fill
it with meaningfulness. No one
you know will accept it, no hard-won
victories anymore, only the struggling.
The next day she rode with him
to the station, sat staid and prim,
only to go on and on about
the bills, accumulating a pout.
He got onto the train after
a stiff peck on the cheek. He left her
again, fondled his bass case
until it sat comfortably in the place
beside him. He tried to feel
good again, forget the idea of home.

Duke Ellington and His Mistress
Make Love

I draw the sheets written with life
around me, expose the concupiscent
figures of my breasts, lips. Your wife
in uncommon laws, I yield to your hands bent
toward my thighs where my life
parts and unveils euphony's scent.

Here in all the hotel rooms,
are the places where we made
spaces for the sound of love on looms.
We rock to the governing grade
of time. It varies only with the boom
of silence. Here I launch your cavalcade.

I tiptoe to where you sit and sing.
I come softly to your head,
as you reckon what string
of notes should begin this bar, be fed
into the stream. Jazz brings
a union to us. The score moves ahead.

I paste my cool hands slowly
to your brow, to test myself.
I see what bandstands or stately
applause shoots through the shelf
of your prescience. Innately,
you feel me blend self to self.

You let your head roll back into
the cradle of my hips, press
your temple and cheek hard to
my navel. I close your eyes, confess
the night of work with a kiss to
your head. Music stirs. We undress.

Duke Ellington Plays to His Mistress

Well past midnight, we kept going
on a thrill that enhanced the night
with sound. We watched the fling
of fifty-cent pieces up to the light
in the ceiling. They had their own
melody to note the people's pleasure
at the hip way we had blown
into tomorrow, measure by measure.
There was a solitary
lady in blue at a front table,
who sipped a little wine delicately
and sniffled. She was unable
to melt into the commotion,
to lose herself in the happy
abandon of celebration.
She couldn't delight in the giddy
roll of early morning wine.
I thought it must be *her,*
again her impossible beauty, fine
and overpowering. With her
I found another burst of magic,
the ability to persevere, to live
another of life's melodic
memories, elusive, explosive.
She used to enrapture me in caresses
she gave me when we were alone.
When she took off her dress
to show her polyvalent tone,
she walked me to a hot bath
with perfumes, scented candles.
I tasted each slender path
of each rhythmic finger to fondle
her with slow adulation.

As I remembered this,
she stopped crying. The attention
brightened her. She blew me a kiss.
I dropped my head to blush,
realized I was doing a solo.
I awoke to give back the rush
of energy to the trumpet.
When I looked up for her,
she had gone, vanished with her table.

Villes Ville

Here they all live,
Bolden, Armstrong,
founders, workers
who move among
a supreme light
that beckons, stirs
where listeners
invoke its sight,
omnipresent
—City of Jazz!

Notes

1. Donald Faulcon and I worked together for ten years in the warehouse of Procter and Gamble's Baltimore plant. Donald was born and raised in North Carolina. As a young boy he lived on the farm of his grandfather, a store owner, near Weldon, North Carolina. I will always remember Donald's tenor voice as he sang "Danny Boy." A musician in his youth, he grew to be a sage and took me into the catacombs of my own mind and human relationships. Donald preferred to be called "Duck" and thus celebrated his iconoclasm. He taught me the pleasure of bicycles and the virtue of black men sitting in silence and peace.

2. In "Sub Shop Girl," Shango and Oshun are deities (orishas) in the Yoruba religion, which originated in what is now known as Nigeria. Oshun's domain includes feminine beauty and coquetry. Shango and Oshun are both highly sexual. Oba means "king" in the Yoruba language.

3. "The Final Trains of August" grew out of my stay at the Open Hearth Motel and Antique Shop in Bar Harbor, Maine, which was owned by Walter and Gertrude Francis. I wrote this poem for them, intending to present it as a gift to them, but when I returned two summers later, I was informed that they died together earlier that spring in a double suicide. Walter was a manic-depressive.

4. The following titles were inspired by compositions by Duke Ellington:

"Rock Skippin' at the Blue Note"
"Blues in Orbit"

"Duke Ellington and His Mistress Make Love"
"Duke Ellington Plays to His Mistress"
"Villes Ville"

5. The following titles were inspired by Duke
Ellington's autobiography, *Music Is My Mistress:*

"Willie 'the Lion' Smith"
"Dancers"
"Billy Strayhorn"
"Sidney Bechet"
"Duke Ellington Remembers Josephine Baker"
"Chicago"
"New York"

6. The following titles were inspired by works by
Jacob Lawrence:

"Harlem Society"
"Parade"
"Street Orator"
"Pool Parlor"
"Jukebox, 1946"
"Bootleg Whiskey for Twenty-five Cents"
"Funeral Sermon, 1946"
"Masks"
"Village Quartet"

7. Indian Pond is a small community in New
Hampshire, fifteen miles from Mt. Washington. In
the summer of 1985, I lived there with Catrina White
(C. W.) in an eighteenth-century farm-house, near Jay
and Lois Wright. That summer formed the crucible of
experience that was the genesis for this collection.

Michael S. Weaver

is a poet, playwright, fiction writer, and freelance journalist. He was born in Baltimore, Maryland. Beginning with his first published poem in 1974, when he was twenty-two, he has gone on to publish individual poems in numerous journals and anthologies. His short fiction can be found in the new edition of the classic anthology *Best Short Stories by Black Writers,* edited by Gloria Naylor. He has had two plays produced professionally, *Rosa,* which was produced in an Equity production by Venture Theatre of Philadelphia, and *Elvira and the Lost Prince,* which received the PDI Award (Playwrights Discovery/Development Initiative) from ETA Creative Arts Foundation in Chicago, Illinois, the largest African-American theater in Chicago.

As a journalist, Weaver's op-eds, book reviews, feature articles, and travel stories have appeared in the *Baltimore Sunpapers, Baltimore Afro-American, City Paper of Baltimore, Philadelphia Inquirer, Boston Globe, Chicago Tribune,* and *Inside Kung-fu.*

In 1986 Mr. Weaver received his B.A. from Regents College (University of the State of New York), and in 1987 he received his M.A. from Brown University. He has received fellowships from the National Endowment for the Arts (1985) and the Pennsylvania Council on the Arts. He teaches at Rutgers University in Camden, New Jersey, and lives in Philadelphia, Pennsylvania.

PITT POETRY SERIES

Ed Ochester, General Editor